The Jesus My Father Showed Me.

The Jesus My Father Showed Me.

Remembering Dad

Jonathan Prox

XULON PRESS

Xulon Press
2301 Lucien Way #415
Maitland, FL 32751
407.339.4217
www.xulonpress.com

Unless otherwise indicated, Scripture quotations taken from the King James Version (KJV)–*public domain.*

Printed in the United States of America.

ISBN-13: 978-1-54566-024-9

Prologue

Someday, I'm going to write a book about my dad and the valuable lessons learned by this godly man. From a very early age, Dad became my best friend, confidante, and mentor. In short, he was my hero.

Dad died a few years back and this book should have been started about sixty years ago, but then that would have made me just three years old. Unfortunately, I've forgotten so much about this man's life.

Anyway, I have decided to start writing now because yesterday, while going through some of his things in an effort to "clean out" some space, I came across a short poem in Dad's handwriting. I found this in his wallet on a 2"x 3" notepad; it speaks loudly about his ability to put his thoughts on paper.

"To My Son"

At first you needed my strong arms, And they were willing too;

God's fatherhood I came to see, When you cuddled close to me.

And then you needed just my hand—A toddler at my side;

How proud you were to stand up straight, And try to match your father's gait!

At last you only sought my voice—A word of counsel kind; You had a body, tall and fine, With strength that far exceeded mine.

And now you have just my prayer—Daily to God I say,

"May this, my son be son of Thine, And hold Thy hand as he held mine."

I don't know if Dad authored this, but I do know he lived it!

I need to tell you that Dad's handwriting was very artistic, with nearly perfect penmanship in his earlier days (one reason why I have saved every letter ever written to me). However, he had lost much of this ability to write due to physical challenges brought on by supra-nuclear palsy, which eventually took his life. From the look of this poem and age of paper, I'm guessing he wrote this in his late thirties or early forties. I would have been about ten years old, my oldest brother about seventeen. He always shared his heart well on paper, and seemed to glorify his Lord with every beat. This is the dad I'd like for you to know, at least a little bit.

I trust and hope that this read will encourage the fathers, and fathers-to-be, out there to help them decide what is really important: to live out their convictions with resolve; to teach their children what really matters in life; and to continue to invest in future generations.

The very foundation and existence of a society depends upon us dads.

DEDICATIONS

THEY SAY BEHIND EVERY GOOD MAN IS A BETTER women. This is the case here, and I dedicate this little book to Mom, the strength of our home. It is you, Mom, who made our home a place of refuge for this scared little boy. It was you, Mom, while sitting on your knee, who opened up the Word of God daily to teach me right from wrong, the "Golden Rule," and the character of God. It was you, Mom who, when I struggled to understand God's word simply said, "Watch your dad."

Thank you so much for those three little words. They say and mean so much now as I realize the effort you put into making our home a godly one. They speak volumes about your heart, your love and trust in God, then in your husband, and then in your family.

I also want to dedicate this book to my sons: Joshua, Eric, and Michael. You are precious in my sight and I have heard you say, "Dad, I hope that I will be half the man you are." Thank you for those kind words, but please don't settle for such a low goal. Set your hearts above to emulate "The Jesus My Father Showed Me." Maybe, someday, your sons will want to write a book.

With much love, honor, and prayer,
Your Son and Father,
Jonathan

Note: Mom died before this was written.

Table of Contents

1

Where Do I Start?

I am sure beginnings are just as important as endings, but Dad taught us all to finish well. Whatever the task we were about to do, do as unto the Lord, seeking His approval first, then continue till the work is done. (Col. 3:23) Wow! This was the first lesson we ever learned from Dad, not only for my sister and two brothers but for everyone who knew him. This virtue was seen and understood the moment you met Dad.

Dad was born into an immigrant family and was the only son with four sisters before him, and five after. When asked about his family, he would respond with a smile on his face, "I've come from a large family… there are nine sisters and every one of them had a brother." He spoke his heart clearly, for every "one" was loved and cared for by him like there was no other. You see, when Dad was twelve years old, his father died of an ear abscess in 1931, leaving his mother, who spoke little English, and ten children. Dad being the only boy, just two years after the Great Depression that lasted for over a decade (and is still known as the worst decade in American history), became the "father of the house."

We read stories of grown men taking their own lives during the Great Depression because of their inability to provide for their families. Dad would just say, "Times were tough," but we have no clue how tough as seen from a scared little twelve-year-old boy with a fresh grave in his memory. I knew Dad became a man that day. He had to put away childish things to survive and he did. He learned to work hard as unto the Lord and "give" when young boys wanted to "get." Working hard to give to others was all Dad knew. I know that giving to others brought him great joy, and I was witness to this fact until the day he died.

By the way, I had never heard Dad complain about anything. The last few years of his life being bedridden, his only concern was that he might be too much of a burden for me. Oh please! Whenever he would voice this concern, it would cause me to think of all the times I couldn't do it right, or got home too late from work when he really needed me, or when I taped mittens on his hands so he couldn't pull on his catheter. I didn't know he was in severe pain from a urinary tract infection when he could not voice the problem. Yet, he never once complained. The Scriptures say that "Contentment is great gain"; well...my dad was the richest man on earth, because he was content.

I learned a lot about the love of God in the face of Dad throughout our years together, but during the last three years, while caring for him, Dad taught me so much more about the grace of God. Oh yeah, Dad finished well.

2

Like Every Dad, He Wanted More For His Children

Even though Dad gave up his childhood to help his family survive, he told many stories about those days in a way that caused me to feel as though I was right there with him. Like the time when he sold newspapers downtown after school to earn what he could at "a penny a pape." He said the walk home was so long and he didn't want to spend any money for a ride, so he would run and catch the back bumper of a trolley and ski the rail out of town, while wearing the soles off his shoes. So as not to get in trouble with his mom for needing new shoes, he would stuff his shoes with a newspaper time and time again to keep on skiing the rails.

There were many more stories like this, and a few more I would like to share, but would rather just say, we wouldn't even comprehend their true meaning today. As Dad worked hard to provide a better life for me, I've done the same for my children and I am sure you are doing the same for yours. Therefore, telling of newspapers in shoes compared to having to have the latest Nike sports shoes just does not compute. Smiles on Dad's face while talking about games like "Kick the Can" versus "Halo 3"; get the picture?! No comparison. In fact, I will go so far as to say, we don't know what "needs" are today. I was spoiled as a child and I have spoiled mine. Yes, spoiled is the right word. Very fitting for us today, and because of this, I think our view of God has been spoiled too.

What I want you to understand is this: Dad would do anything and everything he could, motivated with love, to make our dreams come true, and then lived out his childhood through the smiles on our faces. Let me give you a "for instance."

Since I was eight years old, I knew I was going to be a pilot, and at fifteen I started learning to fly at the local airport, after cutting grass all week long to earn enough money for a one-hour lesson. While friends thought I was nuts for spending all that money in one hour, Dad continued to encourage and support me. I later soloed on my sixteenth birthday, with Dad and Mom as witnesses at the airport. I'll not forget that day. Yet the days and years that followed were long and hard, trying to fill a pilot's logbook for that first rating and getting a private pilot certificate. This certificate only required forty hours of flight experience, but Dad let me earn every penny needed; and at four dollars a yard cutting grass that only grew in the summer, this was my first lesson in perseverance. It wasn't until I was eighteen that I received that precious rating, and guess who was at the airport? You got it. Dad was my very first passenger; another day I will not forget, but here comes the part I really want to share.

About a year later, at nineteen years old and with the excitement of this pilot's license fading off, I found myself in Colorado. I was helping my sister move out there from Shaw AFB, South Carolina as Dad, Mom, and I helped drive the vehicles. While there, I became aware of Black Forest Glider-port and asked Dad if he wanted to go watch the gliders fly. He did, so we went and spent the next hour or so on our backs laying in the grass, watching these sleek high performance sail birds do their dancing in the beautiful Colorado sky. We had one of the best talks a father and son could have. Then out of the blue, Dad said, "Son, I have to go potty." No big deal, I thought, and it's kind of funny now thinking how Dad said that, but that was Dad. So I was left alone to watch and dream a little about floating and soaring like a bird, as those sailplanes made circles in the sky.

Then I heard Dad's voice behind me say, "That's your pilot, right there," speaking of me, and the next thing I knew I was getting into the front seat of a sleek, two-place aerobatic sailplane for the ride of my life, thousands of feet above Pikes Peak, with no sound but my heartbeat coming out of my chest. Now folks, I will never forget this experience as we looped and rolled that plane for what seemed like a million times over some of the most beautiful scenery that God has created; but now, the memory is of a dad who wanted to thrill his son with a ride he would have enjoyed for himself, but couldn't afford. I love you, Dad.

You see, Dad knew how to keep our dreams alive, how to help us stay focused on the goal, and how to run the race of life to win it. It's because of Dad that I have enjoyed a long and prosperous aviation career. This whole story became so clear for me when I had learned that Dad, very late in his years and physically weakened, saw an ultra-light airplane and paid the price for a ride that I knew could not compare to that sailplane. Dad never put himself ahead of us, and he was never far behind. Like his poem, we walked hand in hand all the time.

3

Like Every Dad, He Wanted The Best For His Children

Anything that is good, anything of great value usually comes as a result of a large investment or a lot of hard work, and Dad was not afraid of either. Dad always worked hard and set achievable goals with every task, but more importantly he knew what was worth the effort.

Dad was a good carpenter; not that he wanted to be one, but he realized at a young age he was good with his hands. Working with wood was "natural" for him. However, you won't get rich working in construction, so Dad would always find additional work moonlighting after a long eight hours of labor, and he would take me with him. I don't really remember how old I was, maybe eight or nine, and having worked with my children at this age, I know how frustrating and anti-productive it can be with children at work. However, these memories are the ones I cherish the most.

You see, Dad never made me feel inadequate, unimportant, or "in the way." From the ladder, he would show me a nail and say, "See this, go find me another box of these out of the truck." When I would come back with the wrong ones, he would quietly say, " No, not those; here, take this nail and see if you can match it with the others." After about the third or fourth attempt, he would smile and say, "See, you can do it. Good job, son!" With this kind of encouragement, I soon learned what the difference was from a four-penny and a sixteen-penny nail, a framing verses a finish nail, and every kind of screw in the book. As the days turned into years, we completed some beautiful projects together, but more importantly, he convinced me that I could do anything.

Dad was a hard worker. He knew that providing for the family was at the top of the list, and many of his days were long and way past quitting time, especially during the winter months. This is when most dads would come home, clean up, eat supper, rest a while, then go to bed, and so it was in our house...until it snowed.

It didn't matter if it was a school night or not; if the snow was right and the moon shinning bright, Dad would be shaking you out of bed saying, "Get up, let's go; times a wasting." I can't tell you how many times my two brothers, sister, dad, and I would be sledding down the slopes well past midnight. Of course we were the only ones out there. The sound of silence and moon lit shadows casted on untouched fields of snow, all interrupted with squeals of joy coming from a father with his kids. Yes, Dad would yell the loudest too. In fact, Dad would wear us out before heading home in the early morning hours.

I'd just like to add here, we never used a store-bought sled. Dad built a "special" sled for each one of us that we called a "sit-ski." This was a comfortable stool height seat, built on a single blade runner that could out-maneuver anything on the hill.

To this day I don't understand where Dad got his energy, how he would be rested for the next day of work, but we all knew we were worth it.

4

Like Every Dad, He Loved His Children

I AM SURE MY BROTHERS AND SISTER WOULD LOVE to add to this chapter, because Dad loved us each differently. He understood our strengths and weaknesses, and truly poured himself into each one of us, but Dad also loved "family." Family dynamics were important; in fact, Dad made everyone feel like family. He treated everyone and anyone as if they were somehow in his care to care for, even if it was just for a short time. I am sure that being the "man of the house," caring for his mom and nine sisters in a rural town setting during the thirties and forties was the training ground that made him who he was. He was a strong man and seemed to move with a confidence and an assurance that was unwavering. He was solid, a man's man, and was always in control of his emotions, except this one day.

I will never forget that day when Grandma asked Dad to come to the house. I think it was for his fiftieth birthday and, oddly enough, Dad, Mom, and myself were the only ones to go there. When we walked into Grandma's little kitchen, there was this old, handmade, wicker (rather large) hand basket with a handle and a wicker lid, stuffed full of cash; yes, cash money.

When Dad saw it, he immediately broke down and wept like a baby. Grandma and Dad were hugging each other, talking in Ukrainian and I hadn't a clue what was going on. This was the first time I saw my hero in all his strength, emotionally unravel like a baby.

Dad later explained; "Son, back during World War II, while many were struggling to put food on the table, I left my nine sisters and mom and went to the South Pacific as a Navy Seabee construction worker. I made some good money in those days and would take the cash, stuff it into that basket, and mail it home to my mom, never knowing if it ever got there." Wow. I learned a lot about my dad that day. Dad exercised real faith in people. Can you image sending a lot of cash in an "open to see" wicker basket halfway around the world and hoping it would get there? He did; but in correcting my thoughts, he continued with, "Son, God is the one who blessed me with all that money, so you see it wasn't really my money, but His. So I trusted that God would get it home to help the family." It was this one event that helped me start to understand the man I called Daddy.

You already know he was a hard worker and gave to others, but he had the same dreams that most of us have. He wanted to succeed in his own business and start a construction company. He made some headway and managed to buy about thirteen acres from his uncle and planned to build a housing development to get the ball rolling. Yet his heart always ruled his pocketbook. After building the house I grew up in, he started helping "family" fulfill their dreams too, and I ended up on a dead-end street with sixteen houses, seven of them were built by my aunts and uncles with Dad's help, two Dad built for my grandparents, and one more Dad built for his friend Pon. I am not sure what "Pon" means; I know it wasn't his name, but that's what Dad taught us to call him, and every time we did, it put a smile on his face. Dad met Pon on the streets and learned that he was a widower, as a result of fleeing the Nazi invasion of Russia. He had nothing, couldn't speak English, and had nowhere to go, but Dad spoke Russian, found him a job, and built him a house. In other words, I grew up on a dead-end street with nineteen cousins and every adult looking out for our welfare. Yeah, Dad loved family, and in a very real way, provided for all of us.

During my college years, Dad got me a job working with him in Baltimore where we roomed together during the week at a boarding house. Even though I had to learn how to get to sleep with his snoring, I'll forever treasure this time together. Once I asked him to explain "love." I guess I was wanting a conversation about how to really love someone, but instead, after a short moment of total silence, he said, "Self - Less – Ness," emphasizing each syllable with importance. It's all he said, but it spoke volumes to me. There was no doubt he loved his children.

5

Dad Taught Us The Importance Of Church

My earliest memory of church was getting my ear pinched, to the point of tears, while sitting in a pew, scared to death of making a sound. My heart still smiles at this, as I have always wondered how Dad could reach his arm around Mom with the speed of a serpent and strike with the same accuracy. I'm pretty sure he learned this tactic from his dad, because I know my sons can relate. Anyway, I have many memories from church and most still put a smile on my face. You see, outside of immediate family, church was our life, our joy, our sorrow, and sometime real heartache. "Church" is where we grew up together with fathers, mothers, brothers, sisters, and folks I called aunt and uncle who were strangers just months earlier. In an even deeper way, church was "family" too.

Please understand, Dad built the building (with many members helping in the construction) we called Faith Baptist Church, and we were there faithfully every time the doors were open. Dad was the music leader and sang in a quartet for years. I swear we were the last to leave and lock the doors after every service, but that's really not where I saw Jesus change lives.

Faith Baptist Church is where we heard God's Word preached, but it was at our kitchen table at home where it was lived out.

I mean, it was a rare Sunday night that there wasn't at least a handful of people eating Mom's apple dumplings, talking and sharing about the message and how God was speaking to them. It was here that I saw people sharing their lives together, talking about everyday challenges and hardships, sharing tears and laughter together. It was here at home that prayer filled the rooms and life's victories were won. It was here that I realized the adults in my life were babes at the feet of Jesus. You see, Dad included us kids in his worship of God, where life meets the road, and I got to see a Jesus with skin on. You know what I mean...Real. I was hearing how God changed the lives of others, not because of what Dad said or did. I know with an assurance that it was only God's grace that brought many through the storms of life, but it was Dad that invited folks together in our home; and it was here that I could be an eyewitness. It didn't end on Sunday nights either.

Every Tuesday night during the school year, Mom and Dad hosted a Young Life Club in our living room. In fact, Dad designed our house so that both the living room and the dining room, filled with high-schoolers, could look and listen to the leader standing in front of our fireplace, in what you might call our family room. I know...amazing...right, but what was truly amazing is that there were over two hundred kids in our house at one time, listening to our Young Life leader, Doug talk about Jesus feeding over five thousand with five loaves and two small fishes.

Then on Thursday mornings, Mom would cook breakfast for a dozen or more kids in order to share God's Word and answer questions before heading off to school. You know, I didn't think I was ever going to share this with anyone, and it's rather hard for me to explain now, what it meant to me then, to walk the halls in high school and overhear other students talking about "Aunt Helen and Uncle Pete," knowing that was my mom and dad.

Yeah, I learned what church was: it's the unconditional and limitless love for others that encourages the hearts of all. Only Christ's kind of love can do this, and it's only when we yield ourselves to His will that others will see Jesus with skin on.

By the way, where do you have church?

6

Dad Taught Us How To Forgive

I remember as a child running down the steps and leaping into the living room with stocking feet to slide, as if ice skating across the floor, to see if I could make it to the fireplace. You see, our whole house had tile floors made from a commercial grade vinyl tile of twelve-inch squares. I was the youngest sibling, with my oldest brother seven years my senior, and I know I heard Mom talking about many years living with plain plywood floors before that, so the year Dad put wall-to-wall carpet in was super special. Mom felt like a queen.

However, I remember that year not because Mom felt like royalty, but because within days of the installation Mom and Dad hosted a "fondue party"; you know, one of those parties where you stick a piece of bread or something with a long toothpick and dip it into some hot cheese or boiling oil, or whatever that ugly brown stuff was.

Well, you guessed it, someone had an accident and knocked that pot right off the table onto Mom's brand new carpeting, creating a spot that would remain for the life of those carpets. The guests were kids; kids were always at our house! I don't remember if the culprit cried, but later that night Mom did. Yet when it happened, they treated it like it was no big deal. In fact, Dad wouldn't allow the event to ruin the spirit of the place: hugs were given, songs were sung, and these kids felt an unconditional love that lasted for a long time.

Well, at least it lasted for this kid, because this kind of thing was surely not a one-time event. Why Dad wanted to shellac over our scribbles on our bedroom walls for remembrance sake, but Mom wouldn't have it. Hoorays for Mom, can you imagine having your friends over at sixteen and trying to explain what you did at three?

Anyway, this was my first lesson in how to keep the meaningless things in life meaningless. Do you know the only thing you can take with you after you die are relationships? Dad (and Mom) understood this! This is forgiveness.

Well, accidents and unintentional mistakes are one thing, but what do you do when you are attacked or targeted on purpose? How do you handle the hurts that run deep, the kind that rips your heart out and changes relationships forever? What if it comes from those you love and sacrificed for, like family? Well, to this day I don't know what the event was or what happened to cause it, as I was about eight years old, but it was something very serious because a big part of life changed.

It was about church, and church family. All I knew was suddenly two of my aunts and uncles and six cousins who lived next door stopped coming to my church and went elsewhere. We were close. They say, "blood is thicker than water," and we were "blood." But like I said, I know nothing about it; we still played together every day, rode the bus to school together, ate together on special occasions, and so on. You see, Dad never spoke of the hurt; his only goal was to protect "family," and keep an open house and open arms to everyone. It was my mom's brother and sister who thought it was best to separate their fellowship at church with us. I know this was a painful event for our parents to go through, but we kids never knew. Do you get it? We never knew; that is forgiveness.

Then there was the Soap Box Derby. At fifteen years old, the last qualifying year to compete in the Derby, Dad decided it was my turn to race. My two older brothers, Dave and Ron had their chance, and the excitement was huge after David won the locals five years prior and we all headed to Derby Downs in Akron, Ohio for the Nationals. So Dad helped me build my car, teaching me a lot about the winning design, with drawing after drawing, and about the construction of character: like perseverance over an eight-month build time, patience in getting that finish just right, and endurance with hours of training. He would push me down the street to practice the technique to win the race. We were proud of our car, and Dad was proud of me.

So we loaded up the car and drove to Conshohocken, Pennsylvania for sign-in the night before the race. The officials marveled at our beautiful car; they were amazed by the design and felt sure it was the winning car. Dad and I just smiled on the way home.

The next day started early with an excitement that was hard to describe. We had the immediate and extended family in tow for a day at the races, but when we arrived, my world was about to fall apart. The officials had decided that my car was somehow constructed in an illegal manner and demanded that I took a hacksaw and cut out about forty pounds of weight, which was molded into the car. Weight was everything. This was a gravity race down a hill; a fifteen-year-old understood this. We were careful to follow every rule and Dad disagreed with their decision, but it was "cut the weight out of the car or go home."

With no more words to say, I just looked to Dad as he handed me the saw. I turned to place the saw onto the car and started to cut for just a few seconds when I started crying. My dad and I worked hard together on the car; it meant everything to me. When I turned back to look at Dad, he was crying too. This was the second time I saw Dad cry. This was forgiveness too.

I remember too my first corporate helicopter pilot experience. Although a "corporate" employee, I ended up being a personal helicopter chauffeur for a self-made billionaire. I'll just say it takes a special kind of diplomacy to handle this kind of relationship. My boss surrounded himself with good people, so at first I had great respect for him and felt good about my job, but it took less than a year for the truth to be known.

You see, he loved to sit up front next to me whenever we would fly, and he was always talking to himself out loud, thinking I couldn't hear him with my headset on, but I believe I heard every word. He was a professional deceiver. It was all about money to him: how he could earn it, borrow it, trade for it, or steal it from others. I now understood why my salary was at only sixteen thousand per year. He was the richest man I knew and yet the most unfulfilled man at the same time, but the worst part of it all is that he had many Christian men in the palms of his hands, using them for his advantage. I believe he funded the first Christian satellite television network that made many church leaders seek him out.

One day I flew him to a remote hilltop location, marked only by the four black limousines, where he got out of the helicopter with the instructions to keep it running. I saw men talk, then hug, then have a group prayer. My boss knew I was a Christian, and when he climbed back into the helicopter, he smiled at me and said, "You Christians are so easy; you allow others to control you at a whim." Then he laughed. I knew too much about this man and was way too close to him to feel good about my job any longer. After a short while, I ended up leaving for new employment back home.

Well one day, while spending time with Dad, I started talking about this man in a negative way, like I was trying to bring down judgement onto him in an effort to defend Jesus. My dad wasted no time and was quite firm when he stopped me with, "Son, I don't ever want to hear you talk that way. Never criticize or talk bad about anyone, especially those in authority over you. Speak only to encourage. Take all of your hurts and frustrations to the Lord, and pray for those who persecute you. You go and pray for that man right now, and let God deal with the issues in His own way." Wow, even now as I am writing this, it has come to my mind that I had never heard my dad criticize anyone. I have heard him voice his disappointment about someone, but never attack a person's character. I went and prayed for my previous boss that God would save his soul and fill him with the Holy Spirit. This gave me a "peace unspeakable," and I learned too, this is forgiveness.

So you would think with a dad like this, I would have learned much and would have acquired a mastery of forgiveness. I would love to end this topic right here, but this next story is a must for me, because it is right now that I am asking for forgiveness.

When my wife and I decided to build an addition to our house so that Mom and Dad could move in, we didn't realize how much our lives were going to change. I didn't realize how much their lives have changed. Just let me say, there was a learning curve for us all and it wasn't easy.

I don't know why: maybe her loss of independence, maybe seeing a video of the house you built with your own hands and lived in your entire married life, the house where all these stories are coming from being torn down, or maybe the personal struggles of failing health and battling cancer, but Mom became critical at times and would complain about Dad to dad. You see, Dad was failing in health far beyond Mom's and this too was hard for Mom to deal with. So, to hear Mom complaining to Dad over things he had no control over, like drooling at the table, not being able to fix his own meals, and so on, began to work on me.

I know she didn't mean to sound the way she did, and here's a clear example of what I mean: Dad, with a Parkinson's type of imbalance, would fall hard often. It would so hurt me, because I would not be there to catch him, but Mom would yell, "Peter, why do you do that? Don't fall!" Or, "Peter, stop drooling, you're making a mess!" I know she loved Dad, but it didn't sound like it anymore, and this started to hurt me to the core.

This went on for a while and to the point that my wife started to criticize Mom to me. I became the "man in the middle" and felt myself losing control. Then one day I did.

This was no doubt the darkest day of my life. In the middle of Mom complaining to Dad and yelling at him, I blew up in frustration and started yelling at Mom with curses and hateful speech, totally out of control. My son, who was there, went running scared to his bedroom because of the harshness of words and my tone of voice, but I did all of this right in front of Dad sitting at the table, unable to get up and unable to speak. He should have gotten up and laid me out with one strong punch. I wanted him to get up, but I hardly even noticed him there, as my eyes were focused on Mom in the moment. When I was done, I felt exhausted. My heart was hurting, I was shaking with adrenaline running through my veins, and I felt very much alone. Mom looked shocked and was stunned. Then I turned and looked at Dad...this was the third and last time I ever saw my Dad cry.

"Oh Dad, Mom, please forgive me. I miss you both and wish you were here. Dear Jesus, please let Dad and Mom read this, I love them so much!"

Folks, don't miss the opportunity to forgive. Forgive today, forgive often. How many times? "Seventy times seven!" (Matt. 18:22 KJV)

7

Dad's Love For Jesus Showed

I have been involved with church for over forty-five years, many years as a Sunday School teacher and many as a deacon. I have met several people who profess a commitment to Christ, and many more who say they love Jesus, but I know just a few who show it.

The Bible says, " Out of the heart, man speaketh" (Luke 6:45), good or bad, but James warns us not to be just hearers (or talkers) of the Word, but doers (James 1:22). In other words, "your walk talks louder than your talk talks," and for this reason, I fear for the church today. I see many lifting their "holy hands" in song, which the church now calls "worship" and claiming with our voices that "We love you, Lord. We adore you, Lord, and you are my Lord," but He is not LORD of our lives at all, as evidenced Monday through Saturday. Why most folks give God ninety minutes a week and then act like they know Him?

Well, before I go any further and you start getting the wrong vibes about me, let me remind you of what Jesus had to say about following Him. Jesus said; "Whosoever will come after me, let him deny himself, and take up his cross, and follow me." (Mark 8:34 KJV)

Deny yourself? Have you given thought to what that really means? What areas in my life can I deny myself? This is the first thing we think, yet this is not what Jesus said. I think it means in any and all areas. The apostle Paul speaks much about our gifts and talents that we may have, but that all are worthless if we have not "charity," or love. (1 Cor. 13:1-3) Remember what Dad said when I asked him how to love someone...self-lessness. He lived this way. Others were always ahead of himself.

What about taking up your cross? We understand that a cross is an instrument of death, but somehow we think that this death is a one-time event; yet Jesus said we must take it up and carry it along. He never talks about when we can put it down! I think that in order to deny myself, I must put "MY"-self to death daily, or even many times in a day. Let's face it: our appetites, desires, and wants rule us, whereas Jesus wants to be our Lord.

I have been avoiding the real issue here for a while; Jesus continues with:

> For whosoever will save his life shall lose it; but whosoever shall lose his life for my sake and the gospel's, the same shall save it. For what shall it profit a man, if he shall gain the whole world, and lose his own soul? Or what shall a man give in exchange for his soul? (Mark 8:35-37 KJV)

John the Baptist said it this way, "He (Jesus) must increase, but I must decrease." (John 3:30 KJV) You know, it has been our own demise since the beginning of time, but pride shows its ugly head time and time again. We get frustrated, upset, overwhelmed, angry, and many more negative emotions, all because in some way our pride has been attacked or challenged. I think to deny ourselves really means learning to slay our pride.

Dad did this. I am sure he got frustrated, upset, overwhelmed, and angry, but he was a very humble man and never showed it.

8

Dad Always Had A Smile On His Face

No matter what the forum, time of day, or the company in attendance, when you see someone with a smile, your day gets better. In fact, when a smile stands out of the crowd, you can't help but notice it. Yet for some reason, it must take a lot of work to smile, because few people ever do. Have you ever noticed how painful it is to sing in a church choir? Well, just look at their faces while they're singing "Happy Am I!" I know this sounds funny, but sadly enough you know what I'm saying is true.

Well, Dad loved to smile and he loved to sing. He had a beautiful baritone voice that just begged you to follow along, and he loved to lead people in song. However, whenever he looked out and saw no one smiling, he would stop the music cold, give a loving critique, followed by a pep-talk that caused everyone to laugh into tears. Then the mood was transformed, the music started playing, and the place was filled with true praises to our King, evidenced by the smiles on every heart. Yeah, when your heart smiles, your singing gets much better too.

By the way, it didn't matter if it was at church, a family reunion, a small gathering at home, or even at the funeral home, if there were people gathered, a song would be sung, and Dad knew how to make you smile.

You know, I want to say strangers were gravitated toward Dad because of his smile, but the truth is there were no "strangers" in Dad's mind. Everyone was a friend, and everyone deserved a smile.

9

I Can't Wait To See Dad

By writing this memoir of Dad, my emotions are stirring. I wanted to share those things that would encourage us to see Christ in others, and challenge you with this thought, do others see Christ in you? I have shared memories that made me feel like a little boy, yet I sit here realizing that I am a grandfather. Do my kids see Christ in me? Truth is, I would feel blessed if I could say that I am half the man that my dad was. I wonder if Dad ever felt this way.

Well, a few years ago, while at a family reunion in Myrtle Beach, North Carolina, late one afternoon at sunset, Dad and I were sitting on the beach, just the two of us. This was before Dad came to live with me, but still failing in his health. I started asking questions about heaven.

Now wait, before I share this next story, you need to know that years ago, like a lot of years ago, I asked my dad what his dad was like. To my surprise, his first words were, "I hated him." Then he went on telling me how hard it was to be his son; that his dad was a very strict disciplinarian, with a strong hand and a short temper. The records from Ellis Island said Grand-pop was a tanner by trade, but Dad said he came as a Baptist missionary to the United States to start a Ukrainian-speaking church. He was a pastor and Dad was a "PK," a pastor's kid. Dad said that everyone in the family, he and his nine sisters, had to play a musical instrument for church, forced to play regardless of desire, and that when a wrong note was played, Grand-pop would hit the bell of his trumpet, causing Dad's lips to bleed. This was all Dad said and we never talked about his dad again.

...Now here we are sitting on the beach, and I asked Dad what was the first thing he wanted to do when he got to heaven. He thought a little while, staring at the waves rolling in, and then with tears in his eyes said, "I want to see my dad!" I immediately responded, "Wow! He is going to be so proud of you when he sees you." Then my hero looked at me…and we smiled.

The Bible tells us that this life is like a vapor, here and then gone in a twinkling of the eye, and so it is. (James 4:14) You know; the only things that matter in this life, will matter a thousand years from now. Let that sink in for a minute. I know my dad knew what really mattered.

I have been writing to my sons and to my brothers and sisters in Christ, but maybe you don't know Jesus like we do. Maybe you are struggling to know Him more, or maybe you have a problem with "the church."

I have a friend, Kevin, who I have been witnessing to now for over ten years. We are close friends and trust each other without limits. He reads what I write and encourages me with his every thought. I asked Kevin, "What's the hold-up? Why won't you give your life to Christ?" He looked me in the eyes and said, "If you Christians would stop stabbing each other in the back, I might consider becoming one." Wow! Truth is, my deepest wounds are from Christians. Are we ever going to learn what really matters? Go hug someone today...tell them you love him/her.

Or maybe you might be questioning if this is all real: you know, the Bible, Jesus, heaven and hell. I believe many are trying to deny the fact that they are even dealing with these questions, but one day we all will have to answer to what really matters.

I trust this last chapter will help.

10

I Forgot To Wave Goodbye

First, I want to speak to my brothers and sister. I know we struggled through our decision-making process when considering how to care for Mom and Dad when they would be in need. We talked about nursing homes and other options. Personally, I was praying for the Lord to take Dad home quick, because I was afraid to death I would have to watch as "my hero," in all his physical strength, would slowly fade away. On this subject, and many years ago, Dad explained to me the circle of life. "You come into this world in diapers with no teeth, and you go out the same way."

When we decided to build the addition and have Mom and Dad move in with me and (my wife) Renee, I was terrified! I knew it would be till the end. You all have helped us in many ways to endure, and it wasn't easy. I know you all are very thankful and appreciative of all we have done for them. I came to fully realize this at Dad's funeral service, when brother Ron gave us praises for completing the task. The truth is, I don't feel worthy of any praise. In fact, I feel a little guilt for holding onto the special moments that I have had with Dad during, what I'm going to confess, were the best years of my life. I have been rewarded beyond measure with my fears turning into desire, the honor and joy I felt in caring for the hero we called Daddy, and for experiencing the daily graces of God. I was holding onto this last story selfishly for a personal treasure, but now want to share with you and the world.

Bear with me here for a moment. In 1988, I started a new job as a precast concrete engineer for Concrete Safety Systems in Bethel, Pennsylvania. It was there that I met Melvin Martin. Melvin was an older man and the plant janitor. I quickly befriended him, due to many giving him a hard time with ridicule and slander, and what I thought was unwarranted punishment. As the new guy on campus, I had no idea for the reason of such treatment and Melvin was quite the introvert because of it. It took nearly a year to win his trust and start the conversation.

I learned that Melvin was an ambulance driver and during a recovery to the hospital was t-boned at an intersection and involved in a serious crash. He was pronounced dead at the scene and has a story to tell. He told me what he saw and experienced in heaven.

Now much of his story I will keep as a personal treasure, because it's another book to write and this one is about to end. But I want you to hear this...

..."Jon, when I walked the streets and turned the corners I realized that there were no shadows. Light was everywhere as bright as the sun, but without the strain to gaze upon it. There were buildings of such beauty I cannot define and marvels beyond description! The gardens were full of life, trees yielding all kinds of fruit, and the vineyards rich and full." Then with his hand raised, looking like he was holding a softball, said, "Jon, the grapes are this big!" He went on for hours, but I listened to what I thought were just minutes, and we became eternal friends. But like I said, this was years ago and with the many changes in life and struggles to succeed, an encounter long forgotten.

Now with the end of my story.

The last three months were long days and nights, as Dad could no longer move on his own. I am so grateful for Renee's bedside manners and care, and for the visiting nurses coming twice a week, but I made it a priority to spend the last few hours of each day sitting with Dad and making sure he was ready for the night's sleep. Every time I entered his room, I would be greeted with that smile, and I cherished every one. This is because every time he tried to talk, he would nearly choke to death. It was this way for weeks.

Then to my surprise, I would enter Dad's room time and time again, and he would be talking clearly without effort to someone at the corner of his closet near the ceiling. When he would do this, he would always stare at the same corner of the room. I mentioned this to the nurse, and she discredited it to hallucinations, due to the lack of oxygen in his system from being sedentary. I asked if he needed oxygen, so she put an oxygen sensor on his finger. To our surprise, she said, "No, his oxygen level is great at 89 percent!" Ummm…? Now I couldn't wait to get to Dad every night, just so I could listen in on the conservations.

One time I walked in and Dad was giving instructions to "a man on the roof"; yep, same corner of the room. He, knowing I was there, asked me, " Who is that guy putting on that roof?" I thought for a minute and concluded that as a carpenter all his life, that guy must be doing something wrong and Dad was about to straighten him out. Then at the same moment, I thought Dad was hallucinating. He looked right at me, as if he knew my thought, and said with a gentle smile, "Son, you don't see him, do you?" I lied and said, "Sure I do Dad, what's he doing?" Then Dad smiled again, putting his hand on my shoulder and said, "Oh yeah, what's he wearing?" I was speechless. Then Dad said, "It's okay, son." I said, "You bet it is and I want you to tell me everything you see!"

The last two months were full of conversations with Dad, me, and those I couldn't hear or see. None of which were scary in any way; quite the contrary, they brought a peace with laughter and a clarity to Dad's voice, as if he were young again. One time, Dad said, "Mom, you look so good!" and I wondered if he was seeing heaven.

Then the night before he died, I walked in and Dad was making the motions as if he was eating an imaginary grapefruit like an apple with one hand. I asked him, "What are you doing?" He chewed a few seconds, swallowed and said, "I'm eating grapes!" I responded with, "Are they any good?" He said, "Of course; otherwise I wouldn't be eating them," then kept on chewing. I thought to myself, duh!

The next day, my work schedule allowed me to get home at noon and I wanted to waste no time getting to Dad, but in entering the house, Mom stopped me in the hallway. While she was looking at me from her office door, I was looking at Dad through the hall, smiling at me. Then Mom started to tell me, "Jonathan, I've had a tough day with your dad. I've come to the point where I am asking Jesus to either heal your father now, or take him home." And as Mom was talking, I watched Dad close his eyes and watched as his smile slowly faded away. I immediately hugged Mom and whispered in her ear, "Jesus heard you just now and Dad is gone."

He died in that moment and as Mom went to him, crying softly, I thought...those grapes were good, and forgot to turn and look again to that corner of the room to wave good-bye.

Heaven is for real, folks! Are you going there?

CPSIA information can be obtained
at www.ICGtesting.com
Printed in the USA
BVHW042342031019
560188BV00005B/7/P